This Book Belongs To:

_____

Dear Valued Customer,

Thank you sincerely for choosing to purchase our book!

We're delighted to hear that you've decided to embark on a journey filled with riddles. Our aim is to provide you with an abundance of enjoyment and excitement as you explore the pages ahead. We hope each riddle sparks joy and stimulates your imagination, offering moments of delightful discovery and amusement.

Best wishes on your riddle journey!

What are riddles?

A riddle presents a question that prompts the individual being asked to utilize their intellect and cognitive abilities to respond. Typically, solving a riddle involves thinking "outside of the box" and creatively to uncover the answer.

Example: **What animal is always at a baseball game?**
Answer: **A bat!**

This funny riddle plays on the double meaning of "bat" as both the flying mammal and the equipment used in baseball. It's a clever way to incorporate wordplay into a humorous riddle.

Explore our compilation of funny, easy, and difficult riddles here!
Get ready to stretch your brain muscles and unleash your wit!

If you ever feel stuck,
you can find the answers at the back of the book.

Let the fun begin!

1.	I'm tall when I'm young, and short when I'm old. What am I?
2.	What comes once in a minute, twice in a moment, but never in a thousand years?
3.	What has a head, a tail, is brown, and has no legs?
4.	I can be long or short. I can be grown or bought. I can be painted or left bare. What am I?
5.	I can be cracked, made, told, and played. What am I?
6.	I have keys but open no locks. I have space but no room. You can enter, but you can't go outside. What am I?
7.	What has cities but no houses, forests but no trees, and rivers but no water?

8. I have wings but no feathers. I have a straight path but no direction. What am I?

9. What has a heart that doesn't beat?

10. I speak without a mouth and hear without ears. I have no body, but I come alive with the wind. What am I?

11. What has an endless supply of letters but starts empty every day?

12. What has a neck but no head?

13. I fly without wings. I cry without eyes. Wherever I go, darkness follows me. What am I?

14. What has keys but can't open locks?

15.	I have a face that does not frown. I have hands that do not wave. I have no mouth, but you can hear me.
16.	I go up, and I go down, towards the sky and the ground. I'm present and past tense too, let's go for a ride, me and you.
17.	I'm a word of letters three, add two and fewer there will be.
18.	I'm not alive, but I can grow; I don't have lungs, but I need air.
19.	The more you take, the more you leave behind. What am I?
20.	What has six faces, but does not wear makeup, and twenty-one eyes, but cannot see?
21.	I'm often running yet have no legs. You need me, but I don't need you. What am I?

22. I'm taken from a mine, and shut up in a wooden case, from which I'm never released, and yet I am used by almost every person. What am I?

23. What has eyes but can't see?

24. I'm always in front of you, but you'll never see me. What am I?

25. Kids can make it but never hold it or see it. What is it?

26. I'm black and white and loved all over China. What am I?

27. All about, but cannot be seen,
Can be captured, cannot be held,
No throat, but can be heard.

28. I'm full of holes, yet I'm full of water. What am I?

29. What always runs but never walks, often murmurs, never talks, has a bed but never sleeps, has a mouth but never eats?

30. At night they come without being fetched. By day they are lost without being stolen. What are they?

31. The more you have of it, the less you see. What is it?

32. What English word has three consecutive double letters?

33. What's black when you get it, red when you use it, and white when you're all through with it?

34. You throw away the outside and cook the inside. Then you eat the outside and throw away the inside. What did you eat?

35. Which letter of the alphabet has the most water?

36. I am always hungry,
I must always be fed.
The finger I touch,
Will soon turn red.

37. I am the beginning of the end, and the end of time and space. I am essential to creation, and I surround every place. What am I?

38. Until I am measured I am not known,
Yet how you miss me when I have flown.

39. When set loose, I fly away,
Never so cursed as when I go astray.

40. Lighter than what I am made of,
More of me is hidden than is seen.

41. Each morning I appear to lie at your feet,
All day I will follow no matter how fast you run, yet I nearly perish in the midday sun.

42.	My life can be measured in hours, I serve by being devoured. Thin, I am quick, Fat, I am slow, Wind is my foe.
43.	I am seen in the water if seen in the sky, I am in the rainbow, a jay's feather, and lapis lazuli.
44.	Glittering points that downward thrust, Sparkling spears that never rust.
45.	You heard me before, yet you hear me again, Then I disappear, 'till you call me again.
46.	At the sound of me, men may dream or stamp their feet, At the sound of me, women may laugh or sometimes weep.
47.	It cannot be seen, it weighs nothing, but when put into a barrel, it makes it lighter. What is it?

48. I build up castles.
I tear down mountains.
I make some men blind,
I help others to see.
What am I?

49. Two in a corner, 1 in a room, 0 in a house, but 1 in a shelter. What am I?

50. What happens when you throw a yellow rock into a purple stream?

51. What starts with a T, ends with a T, and has T in it?

52. You saw me where I never was and where I could not be. And yet within that very place, my face you often see. What am I?

53. Say my name and I disappear.
What am I?

54.	What is it that after you take away the whole, some still remains?
55.	A box without hinges, lock or key, yet golden treasure lies within. What is it?
56.	Forward I'm heavy, but backwards I'm not. What am I?
57.	Why doesn't a mountain covered with snow catch cold?
58.	I can be long, or I can be short. I can be grown, and I can be bought. I can be painted, or left bare. I can be round, or square. What am I?
59.	One by one we fall from heaven down into the depths of past, and our world is ever upturned so that yet some time we'll last.

60. Kings and queens may cling to power, and the jesters may have their call. I am the most common, But I can rule them all. What am I?

61. Soft and fragile is my skin,
I get my growth in mud.
I'm dangerous as much as pretty,
For if not careful, I draw blood.

62. My first is twice in apple but not once in tart. My second is in liver but not in heart. My third is in giant and also in ghost. Whole I'm best when I am roast. What am I?

63. What gets wetter as it dries?

64. When you went into the woods, you got me. You hated me, yet you wanted to find me. You went home with me cause you couldn't find me. What am I?

65. An iron horse with a flaxen tail. The faster the horse runs, the shorter his tail becomes. What is it?

66. You have to travel far before you turn it over. What is it?

67. A mile from end to end,
Yet as close to as a friend.
A precious commodity, freely given.
Seen on the dead and on the living.
Found on the rich, poor, short and tall,
But shared among children most of all.
What is it?

68. What is in seasons, seconds, centuries and minutes but not in decades, years or days?

69. It's red, blue, purple and green,
no one can reach it, not even the queen.
What is it?

70. Plow and hoe, reap and sow,
What soon does every farmer grow?

71. What building has the most stories?

72. A man went to the hardware store
to buy items for his house.
1 would cost $0.25.
12 would cost $0.50.
122 would cost $0.75.
When he left the store he had spent $0.75.
What did he buy?

73. What makes a loud noise when changing its
jacket, becomes larger but weighs less?

74. I called my dog from the opposite side of the
river. The dog crossed the river without
getting wet, and without using a bridge,
a boat, or a raft. How is that possible?

75. What gets broken without being held?

76.
This thing all things devours:
Birds, beasts, trees, flowers;
Gnaws iron, bites steel;
Grinds hard stones to meal;
Slays king, ruins town,
And beats high mountain down.
What am I?

77.
There is a house. One enters it blind and comes out seeing. What is it?

78.
I can trap many different things and colors, ever changing, not boring. Look closely and you may find yourself also caught in my trap.

79.
Pregnant every time you see her,
Yet she never will give birth.

80.
I go around in circles,
But always straight ahead
Never complain,
No matter where I am led.

81. When you need me, you throw me away. But when you're done with me, you bring me back. What am I?

82. What can travel around the world while staying in a corner?

83. What has a face and two hands but no arms or legs?

84. What does a house wear?

85. What time is it when an elephant sits on a fence?

86. What can you see in the middle of the sea?

87. Where would you take a sick boat?

88. What creature is smarter than a talking parrot?

89. What rock group consists of four famous men, but none of them sing?

90. How does a bee get to school?

91. I give milk, and I have a horn, but I'm not a cow. What am I?

92. What is 3/7 chicken, 2/3 cat, and 2/4 goat?

93. Why did Tigger go to the bathroom?

94. Why is England the wettest country?

95. Stealthy as a shadow in the dead of night, cunning but affectionate if given a bite. Never owned but often loved. At my sport considered cruel, but that's because you never know me at all.

96. I have no sword, I have no spear, yet rule a horde which many fear, my soldiers fight with wicked sting, I rule with might, yet am no king. What am I?

97. I am fun and sad. I am fast and slow. I get louder and I get softer. And I am created by great geniuses. What am I?

98. Thirty white horses on a red hill, first they champ, then they stamp, then they stand still.

99. I weaken all men for hours each day. I show you strange visions while you are away. I take you by night, by day take you back. None suffer to have me, but do from my lack. What am I?

100.	Why did the skeleton not go to the party?
101.	What type of music do rabbits listen to?
102.	What can make the octopus laugh?
103.	I am a strange creature, hovering in the air, Moving from here to there, with a brilliant flare. Some say I sing, but others say I have no voice, so I just hum, as a matter of choice.
104.	The strangest creature you'll ever find: Two eyes in front and many more behind.
105.	If a man would carry my burden, He would break his back. I am not rich But leave silver in my track.
106.	Which vehicle is spelled the same forwards and backwards?

107. Where force can't get through, I with a gentle movement do. What am I?

108. I can be flipped and broken but I never move. I can be closed, and opened, and sometimes removed. I am sealed by hands. What am I?

109. To give me to someone I don't belong to is cowardly, but to take me is noble. I can be a game, but there are no winners. What am I?

110. What can you hold in your left hand and not in your right?

111. Why is 6 afraid of 7?

112. If an electric train is traveling south, which way is the smoke going?

113. What does a rich man need that a poor man has?

114.	Turn me on my side and I am everything. Cut me in half and I am nothing. What am I?
115.	I contain words about words, some of which you've never heard. What am I?
116.	What are the next three letters in this combination: OTTFFSS?
117.	Which English verb becomes past tense just by rearranging the letters?
118.	I am lighter than air, But a hundred people cannot lift me. Careful, I am fragile. What am I?
119.	How high do you have to count before you use the letter "a" in the English spelling of the whole number?
120.	What is the saddest fruit?

121. What has 5 fingers but is not alive?

122. I am laced twice in eternity and always within sight. What am I?

123. What has a tongue but cannot talk?

124. What is easier to get into than out of?

125. What always ends up broken before you use it?

126. If you threw a yellow stone into a blue sea, what would it become?

127. What number is odd until you take away one letter; then it becomes even?

128.	There is one word spelled wrong in every English dictionary. What is it?
129.	I sometimes run but cannot walk. You follow me around. What am I?
130.	What word begins and ends with "e" but only has one letter?
131.	What do you find at the end of a rainbow?
132.	I give you one, and you have two or none. What am I?
133.	What has 1000 needles but cannot sew?
134.	How many months of the year have 28 days?
135.	I am a kind of coat that can only be put on when wet. What am I?

136.	What bank never has any money?
137.	When is "L" greater than "XL"?
138.	What is the pet that always stays on the floor?
139.	What is as big as a hippo but weighs nothing at all?
140.	How do you make the number "one" disappear?
141.	What type of cheese is made backward?
42.	There was a blue one-story house in a nice neighborhood. Everything in it was blue — the walls, the carpets, the furniture, even the dog! What color were the stairs?
43.	What did the stamp say to the envelope on Valentine's Day?

144.	What did one volcano say to the other?
145.	What has an eye but cannot see?
146.	I'm a slippery fish in a cloudy sea; Neither hook nor spear will capture me; With your hand you must hunt down this fish, to see that it ends up in the dish.
147.	What is the wealthiest nut?
148.	What do you get when you cross an automobile with a household animal?
149.	It doesn't live within a house, nor does it live without. Most will use it when they come in, and again when they go out.
150.	A cowboy rode into town on Friday. He stayed for three nights and rode out on Friday. How is this possible?

151. I am easy to lift, but hard to throw. What am I?

152. I welcome the day with a show of light, I stealthily came here in the night. I bathe the earthy stuff at dawn, But by noon, alas! I'm gone.

153. How do you spell COW in thirteen letters?

154. Why is Europe like a frying pan?

155. What 5-letter word typed in all capital letters can be read the same upside down?

156. Which fish costs the most?

157. David's father has three sons: Snap, Crackle, and _____?

158. What should you tell a snowman after saying goodbye?

159.	**What kind of tree can you carry in your hand?**
160.	**I love to dance, and twist. I shake my tail as I sail away. When I fly wingless into the sky. What am I?**
161.	**What goes up but never comes down?**
162.	**You'll find me in Mercury, Earth, Mars, Jupiter, Saturn, and Uranus. But never Neptune, or Venus. What am I?**
163.	**Long legs, crooked thighs, little head, and no eyes. What am I?**
164.	**One strand dangles. Two strands twist. Three or more can fashion this.**
165.	**What can fill a room but takes up no space?**
166.	**What is always on its way but never arrives?**

25

167.	Though blind as well, can lead the blind well. What am I?
168.	What can bring back the dead; Make us cry, make us laugh, make us young. Born in an instant yet lasts a life time?
169.	What can go through glass without breaking it?
170.	It belongs to you, but other people use it more than you do. What is it?
171.	What has a big mouth, yet never speaks?
172.	What has roots that nobody sees, Is taller than trees, Up, up it goes, Yet it never grows?
173.	What gets bigger the more you take away?
174.	Remove 'Y' and you do this with apparel. Remove 'E' and I am cautious.

175.	What is made of wood but can't be sawed?
176.	What goes through cities and fields but never moves?
177.	What is always old and sometimes new; never sad, sometimes blue; never empty, but sometimes full; never pushes, always pulls?
178.	There is an ancient invention, still used in some parts of the world today, that allows people to see through walls. What is it?
179.	What can be touched but can't be seen?
180.	It's shorter than the rest, but when you're happy, you raise it up like it's the best. What is it?
181.	I have a face, yet no senses. But I don't really care, because time is of the essence. What am I?

182. I bind it, and it walks. I loose it and it stops. What is it?

183. It stands on one leg with its heart in its head. What is it?

184. What has its heart in its head?

185. What can be held without using your hands or arms?

186. Take one out and scratch my head, I am now black but once was red. What am I?

187. I am black when I am clean and white when I am dirty. What am I?

188. The sun bakes them, the hand breaks them, the foot treads on them, and the mouth tastes them. What are they?

189. Many hear me, but no one sees me, and I only speak when spoken to. What am I?

190.	I fly through the air on small feathered wings, seeking out life and destroying all things.
191.	What has 4 eyes but can't see?
192.	I make you weak at the worst of all times. I keep you safe, I keep you fine. I make your hands sweat. And your heart grow cold. I visit the weak, but seldom the bold.
193.	What is often returned, but never borrowed?
194.	What word is the same written forward, backward and upside down?
195.	When it is alive we sing, when it is dead we clap our hands. What is it?
196.	What do people want the least on their hands?
197.	A girl was ten on her last birthday, and will be twelve on her next birthday. How is this possible?

198.	What never asks a question but is answered?
199.	Walk on the living, they don't even mumble. Walk on the dead, they mutter and grumble. What are they?
200.	It floats over the land, it cuts the tallest mountain, its voice is like a fountain, its body like a snake, will flow into a lake.
201.	What jumps when it walks and sits when it stands?
202.	What animal keeps the best time?
203.	You answer me, but I never ask you a question. What am I?
204.	What is so fragile that saying its name breaks it?
205.	Large as a mountain, small as a pea, Endlessly swimming in a water-less sea.

206.	I fly all day long but don't go anywhere. What am I?
207.	What can be forever wound up but never annoyed?
208.	I have a hundred legs, but cannot stand. I have a long neck, but no head. I cannot see. I'm neat and tidy as can be. What am I?
209.	Blend a teapot shot, so the pearlies won't rot! What am I?
210.	Has no feet, but travels far. Is literate, but not a scholar. Has no mouth, yet clearly speaks.
211.	I can be short and sometimes hot. When displayed, I rarely impress. What am I?
212.	In Paris but not in France, the thinnest of its siblings. What is it?
213.	They're big and blue, and larger than seas. What are they?

214. My head bobs lazily in the sun. You think I'm cute. For my face is yellow my hair is white and my body is green. What am I?

215. What is it that everybody does at the same time?

216. I sleep by day, I fly by night. I have no feathers to aid my flight. What am I?

217. If Teresa's daughter is my daughter's mother, who am I to Teresa?

218. It is worldwide, but once only a spider could weave one. What is it?

219. What can you catch but never throw?

220. What has many teeth but cannot bite?

221. Two fathers and two sons are in a car, yet there are only three people in the car. How?

222.	A bus driver goes the wrong way down a one-way street. He passes the cops, but they don't stop him. Why?
223.	Where is the only place where today comes before yesterday?
224.	It's the only vegetable or fruit that is never sold frozen, canned, processed, cooked, or in any other form but fresh.
225.	You can spin, wheel and twist, but this thing can turn without moving.
226.	A beggar's brother went out to sea and drowned. But the man who drowned had no brother. Who was the beggar to the man who drowned?
227.	I have split the one into five. I am the circle that few will spy. I am the path that breaks and gives. I am the bow no man may bend.
228.	What has a spot and is very bright, is sometimes, red, white, blue, yellow, or green and is often blinding?

229. I wear a green jacket on the outside white jacket as a second layer and red jacket inside. I am pregnant with a lot of babies. What am I?

230. From house to house I go, sometimes narrow, sometimes wide. And whether there's rain or snow I always stay outside. What am I?

231. A house with two occupants, sometimes one, rarely three. Break the walls, eat the borders, then throw away me. What am I?

232. What won't break if you throw it off the highest building in the world, but will break if you place it in the ocean?

233. You can collect me, and you can toss me, you can flip me, you can spin me, and people all around the world have different versions of me. What am I?

234. In what year did Christmas Day and New Year's Day fall in the same year?

235.	What is the question you can ask all day, get different answers for the same, and they would still be correct?
236.	An elephant in Africa is called Lala. An elephant in Asia is called Lulu. What do you call an elephant in Antarctica?
237.	What is deaf, dumb and blind and always tells the truth ?
238.	Deep, deep, do they go. Spreading out as they go. Never needing any air. They are sometimes as fine as hair.
239.	Why is the letter 't' like an island?
240.	They are many and one, they wave and they drum, used to cover a stare, they go with you everywhere.
241.	What's right and never wrong?

242. What surrounds the world, yet dwells within a thimble?

243. I bubble and laugh, and spit water in your face. I am no lady, and I don't wear lace. What am I?

244. Two bodies have I, though both joined in one, The more I stand still the faster I run. What am I?

245. A warrior amongst the flowers, he bears a thrusting sword. Able and ready to use, to guard his golden hoard.

246. Runs smoother than any rhyme, loves to fall but cannot climb!

247. What flies when it's born, lies when it's alive, and runs when it's dead?

248. Name three keys that unlock no doors.

249. I'm always there, some distance away. Somewhere between land or sea and sky I lay. You may move towards me, yet distant I stay. What am I?

250. What do cinders, charcoal, ember, and fire have that a smoke simply doesn't have?

251. A skin have I, more eyes than one. I can be very nice when I am done. What am I?

252. What do you have when twenty rabbits step backwards?

253. As I was going to St. Ives, I met a man with seven wives, the seven wives had seven sacks, the seven sacks had seven cats, the seven cats had seven kittens; kittens, cats, sacks and wives, how many were going to St. Ives?

254. What did the ocean say to the sea?

255.	What time is it when 12 cats chase a mouse?
256.	I'm the source of all emotion, but I'm caged in a white prison. What am I?
257.	What can pass before the sun without making a shadow?
258.	Mountains will crumble and temples will fall. And no man can survive its endless call.
259.	What bird can lift the heaviest weight?
260.	This is in a realm of true and in a realm false, but you experience me as you turn and toss. What am I?
261.	I have four wings, but cannot fly, I never laugh and never cry; On the same spot, I'm always found, toiling away with little sound. What am I?

262.	I can be found in water but never wet. What am I?
263.	People make me, save me, change me, and raise me. What am I?
264.	Some will use me, others not. Some have remembered, others forgot. For profit or gain, I'm used expertly. I can't be picked off the ground or tossed into the sea. What am I?
265.	Where can happiness always be found?
266.	What did the zero say to the eight?
267.	I have strong affection for belly buttons. What am I?
268.	What is it that smells most in a perfume shop?

269.	What is the best thing to put into pies?
270.	I am your most powerful weapon; I come before your eyes. I help you seek the truth, yet I often give you lies. What am I?
271.	You hear me speak, for I have a hard tongue. But I cannot breathe, for I have not a lung. What am I?
272.	What walks on four legs in the morning, two legs in the afternoon, three legs in the evening, and no legs at night?
273.	What is shaped like a box, has no feet, and runs up and down?
274.	What do you call a sleeping bull?
275.	A young man wants to have it, but when he has it, he no longer wants it. Blade in hand, he attacks it and does his best to remove it. Yet he knows that it is all in vain. What is it?

276.	My voice is tender, my waist is slender, and I'm often invited to play. Yet wherever I go, I must take my bow or else I have nothing to say. What am I?
277.	You see a boat filled with people. It has not sunk, but when you look again, you don't see a single person on the boat. Why?
278.	What loses its head in the morning and gets it back at night?
279.	I am bought by the yard but worn by the foot. What am I?
280.	I never was but always will be. No one ever saw me but everyone knows I exist. I give people the motivation to better themselves every day. What am I?
281.	I am a cave full of bones and the house of a worm. What am I?
282.	I belong to everyone. Sometimes make you happy, sometimes make you sad. I will never end until the day you do.

283. I give life for my own, have a beginning, but my end is unknown. What am I?

284. We are all around, yet to us, you are half blind. Sunlight makes us invisible and difficult to find. What are we?

285. What do Alexander The Great and Winnie The Pooh have in common?

286. I run, it runs. I stop, it still runs. What is it?

287. I'm not really more than holes tied to more holes; I'm strong as good steel, though not as stiff as a pole.

288. Everyone in the world needs me. They generously give me but never take me. What am I?

289. What is harder to catch the faster you run?

290.	What side of a cat has the most fur?
291.	A man goes out in heavy rain with nothing to protect him from it. His hair doesn't get wet. How does he do that?
292.	I am the kind of soda you must not drink. What am I?
293.	Born of sorrow, grows with age, you need a lot to be a sage. What is it?
294.	A butcher is 6 feet tall and wears size 12 shoes. What does he weigh?
295.	What do you get when you cross a snowman with a vampire?
296.	I can be driven, but have no wheels. I can be sliced, but still remains whole. What am I?

297. I can swim but never get wet.
I can run but never get tired.
I follow you everywhere
But never say a word. What am I?

298. I am the key that is the hardest to turn. What am I?

299. What has four wheels and flies?

300. Who spends the day at the window, goes to the table for meals, and hides at night?

301. Three different doctors said that Paul is their brother, yet Paul claims he has no brothers. Who is lying?

302. What is it that no one wants, but no one wants to lose?

303. How can you physically stand behind your father while he is standing behind you?

304.	I have 13 hearts but no lungs or stomach. What am I?
305.	I am something people love or hate. I change people's appearances and thoughts. If a person takes care of themselves, I will go up even higher. Some people might want to try and hide me, but I will show. No matter how hard people try, I will never go down. What am I?
306.	First you eat me, then you get eaten. What am I?
307.	After you go through a fall I will take over. All life will stall, or at least grow slower. What am I?
308.	I have a frame but no pictures. I have poles but not standing up. What am I?

309. You go at red and stop at green. What am I?

310. Nobody has ever walked this way. Which way is it?

311. You are my brother, but I am not your brother. Who am I?

312. I have many faces, expressions, and emotions, and I am usually right at your fingertips. What am I?

313. I belong in December, but not in any other month. I am not a holiday. What am I?

314. My thunder comes before the lightning. My lightning comes before the clouds. My rain dries all the land it touches. What am I?

315. What goes up a chimney down But can't come down a chimney up?

316.	How is seven different from the rest of the numbers between one and ten?
317.	You're in a dark room with a candle, A wood stove, and a gas lamp. You only have one match, So what do you light first?
318.	What has ten letters and starts with gas?
319.	Which weighs more, a pound of feathers or a pound of bricks?
320.	What is the longest word in the dictionary?
321.	What word becomes shorter when you add two letters to it?
322.	What has only two words, but thousands of letters?
323.	There are 6 sisters. Each sister has 1 brother How many brothers are in the sister's family?

324.	What English word retains the same pronunciation, even after you take away four of its five letters?
325.	I am served at a table, in gatherings of two or four. Served small, white, and round. You'll love some, and that's part of the fun. What am I?
326.	I can shave everyday, but my beard never changes. What am I?
327.	If a plane came crashing down on the border between Canada and America, where are the survivors buried?
328.	During what month do people sleep the least?
329.	Ten ladies tried to fit under a small umbrella, none of them got wet. How did they do it?
330.	What goes up when rain comes down?

331.	What goes up and down but never moves?
332.	I look at you, you look at me. I raise my right, you raise your left. What am I?
333.	Take it and you will lose or gain more than the others.
334.	Two fathers and two sons are in a car, yet there are only three people in the car. How is this possible?
335.	Though not a plant, I have leaves. Though not a beast, I have spine. Though many wouldn't need me, I am more valuable than wine.
336.	I stare at you, you stare at me. I have three eyes, yet can't see. Every time I blink, I give you commands. You do as you are told, with your feet and hands. What am I?

337. I have an eye but cannot see. I'm faster than any man alive and have no limbs. What am I?

338. Weight in my belly, trees on my back. Nails in my ribs, feet I do lack. What am I?

339. I cover what is real and hide what is true, But sometimes I bring out the courage in you. What am I?

340. Above the kingdom I reign, spotted, speckled, with a mane, I travel in packs, And if you're lucky, you'd ride me. What am I?

341. When you do not know what I am, then I am something. But when you know what I am, then I am nothing. What am I?

342. A large oasis in the desert. Come with cash and leave with none. What am I?

343. Two legs I have, and this will confound, only at rest do they touch the ground. What am I?

344. I have a leg but I do not move,
A face but no expression,
Be it wind or rain I stay outside.
What am I?

345. Always well dressed, but I never fly.
Black and white, sometimes in a tie.
I swim and slide, and dance and glide,
With one person by my side. What am I?

346. Without a bridle, or a saddle, across a thing
I ride astraddle. And those I ride,
by help of me, though almost blind,
are made to see. What am I?

347. I have four legs, a back, but no head.
What am I?

348. I'm named after nothing,
Though I'm awfully clamorous.
And when I'm not working,
Your house is less glamorous. What am I?

349. Full of dark, filled with everything
Both on my skin they color
With my pack, I am always
afraid of the cat. What am I?

350. Although I'm far from the point,
I'm not a mistake. I fix yours.

351. I cut through evil like a double edged
sword, and chaos flees at my approach.
Balance I singlehandedly upraise,
through battles fought with heart and mind,
Instead of with my gaze. What am I?

352. One simple click, one simple flash.
A piece of memory, for years I'll last.
What am I?

353. I work hard most every day,
Not much time to dance and play,
If I could reach what I desire,
All like me would now retire. What am I?

354. A long snake that smokes. What am I?

355.	To unravel me, you need a key. No key that was made by locksmith's hand, but a key that only I will understand. What am I?
356.	I don't exist unless you cut me, But if you stab me I won't bleed. I hate no one yet am abhorred by all. What am I?
357.	I am something all men have but all men deny. Man created me but no man can hold me. What am I?
358.	I have many ears, this may be true. But no matter how you shout, I'll never hear you. What am I?
359.	I warn you about meetings, and I assist you in your life, I can help you do most of your work, unless I have a bug. What am I?
360.	I fall with the waves, rise with the tide, and drift with the current alongside. What am I?

361. You may have many of me but never enough. After the last one arrives, you will have no more. What am I?

362. When they are caught, they are thrown away. When they escape, you itch all day.

363. I am rubber you can eat. What am I?

364. Born from a fountain of wealth, I am black instead of gold but valued the same. What am I?

365. A book once owned by the wealthy, now rare to find. Never for sale and often left behind. What am I?

366. I am a caribbean shape that makes ships disappear. What am I?

367. A hand without flesh and nothing can I hold. My grip cannot be used until I am sold. What am I?

368.	I moan, I groan, I chase after you. I never seem to rest. Time's up for you. What am I?
369.	People need me, yet they give me away every day. What am I?
370.	I do not eat food. But I do enjoy a light meal everyday. What am I?
371.	I am an insect, half of my name is another insect. I am similar to the name of a famous band. What am I?
372.	A container holding water but not a cup. If you want to find me, look up. What am I?
373.	I'll shout 'til you wake or sing you to sleep. I'll talk to you, but you're crazy if you talk back. What am I?
374.	I was not born, but I am here. I have no name, but I am given many. I was made by science and life. What am I?

375. I only exist when you are here.
Where you never were, I can never be.

376. I am a protector. I sit on a bridge.
One person can see right through me,
While others wonder what I hide.
What am I?

377. Secured in place, I work undercover,
And with a flick of your finger,
My purpose you'll discover.

378. I am a man without bones,
Without blood, without life.
My flesh is white, cold and shrinking.
What am I?

379. Black within and red without,
With four corners round about.
What am I?

380. I am sometimes yellow and sometimes
white. Half of me is dark and the other
is light. What am I?

381. From that which comes within itself,
It builds its table on my shelf.

382.	Three little letters, a paradox to some. The worse that it is, the better it becomes.
383.	Useful tool for who in darkness dwell. Within you, corrupting like a deadly spell.
384.	I can wake you up in the morning, but I require no electricity or winding. What am I?
385.	Step on me and you'll reach the top first, but step under me and you're cursed. What am I?
386.	I remain unseen but hold many things, and when you are making a decision, you consult me. What am I?
387.	I am free the first time and second time, but the third time is going to cost you money. What am I?
388.	I have no bones and no legs, But if you keep me warm, I will soon walk away. What am I?

389. I am a king but also a common device of measure. What am I?

390. You hold my tail while I fish for you. What am I?

391. I save lives on the ground and in the air. What am I?

392. A hole in a pole. Though I fill a hole in white, I'm used more by the day and less by the night. What am I?

393. Round as a button, deep as a well. If you want me to talk, you must first pull my tail. What am I?

394. You take my clothes off when you put your clothes on. What am I?

395. How can a person go about 26 days without sleep?

396. You must keep this thing,
Its loss will affect your brothers.
For once yours is lost,
It will soon be lost by others. What is it?

397. For most, I am fast.
For others, I am slow.
An obsession to all,
I make the world go. What am I?

398. I look like a tiny trombone. What am I?

399. I make things short,
But I am pretty long myself. What am I?

400. I can be found on a present, the front of a boat, or after the rain. What am I?

401. I can wave my hands at you, but I never say goodbye. You are always cool when with me, even more so when I am high! What am I?

402. My first two letters say my name.
My last letter asks a question.
What I embrace I destroy. What am I?

403.	What has no beginning, end, or middle?
404.	I am a fire's best friend. When fat, my body fills with wind. When pushed too thin, Through my nose I blow. Then you can watch the embers glow. What am I?
405.	I crawl on the earth and rise on a pillar. What am I?
406.	When I point up it's bright, but when I point down it's dark. What am I?
407.	What gets broken when you don't hold it?
408.	I am the most famous dinner. What am I?
409.	Some people avoid me, some people count me, some people just consume me. What am I?

410.	I am young in the sun and trapped to be aged. Held in a bottle but opening is delayed. What am I?
411.	I start new then become old. Start clean but be one dirty. I usually start big then become little. What am I?
412.	With three eyes and a black as night, I frequently knock down ten men with a single strike! What am I?
413.	Often held but never touched, always wet but never rusts, often bites but seldom bit, to use me well you must have wit. What am I?
414.	Tucked out of sight. I sing best at night. No instrument around, but you'll find me on the ground. What am I?
415.	I am round. I have only one line. Circle is not my name indeed. What am I?
416.	Without me where would you be? I am not your eyes, but I help you see. What am I?

417. I have a head but no body,
A heart but no blood.
Just leaves and no branches,
I grow without wood. What am I?

418. I may be made of metal, bone, or wood
and have many teeth. My bite hurts no one,
and the ladies love me.

419. On the wall, in the air,
You just want me out of your hair,
Try to catch me, but you cannot,
For my vision is thousand fold.

420. A man and his boss have the same parents
but are not siblings. How is this possible?

421. I am long and thin and make things right.
I will repair your mistake but watch my bite.
What am I?

422. I come in many shapes, sizes, and colors.
I stick to many surfaces but I am, in fact,
not sticky at all. What am I?

423. I am a ship that can be made to ride the greatest waves. I am not built by objects, but built by minds. What am I?

424. A necessity to some, a treasure to many, I'm best enjoyed among pleasant company. Some like me hot, some like me cold. Some prefer mild, some like me bold. What am I?

425. Never resting, never still.
Moving silently from hill to hill.
It does not walk, run or trot.
All is cool where it is not.

426. I am a mountain at night, meadow at day. What am I?

427. I am mother and father, but never birth or nurse. I'm rarely still, but I never wander. What am I?

428. I can never be stolen from you.
I am owned by everyone.
Some have more, some have less.
What am I?

429. I give people a huge fright, but at the end, I'm sweet. I normally celebrate at night, when there's less heat. What am I?

430. I count time, but have no end. Tick tick, but I am not a clock. What am I?

431. I can be entertaining until you realize some pieces have been lost. What am I?

432. Tickle with your fingers and a song it will sing. Be careful, though, you may break a string. What is it?

433. My treasures are golden and guarded by thousands amongst a maze no man can enter. What am I?

434. I enclose you in darkness but allow you to see many things. If you resist me, you're likely to get rings. What am I?

435. Everybody has some. You can lose some, you can gain some. But you cannot live without it. What am I?

436.	I can be simple or I can be complex. I can be found in this riddle or in everyday life. I can be shapes or even colors. What am I?
437.	I run distances, often making many turns, yet I never move one foot. What am I?
438.	No matter how little or how much you use me, you change me every month. What am I?
439.	Though learning has fed me, I know not a letter; I live among the books, Yet am never the better. What am I?
440.	I climb higher as I get hotter. I can never escape from my crystal cage. What am I?
441.	I am free for the taking. Through all of your life, though given but once at birth. I am less than nothing in weight, but will fell the strongest of you if held. What am I?

442. I encourage people to run home and steal. What am I?

443. I am wood that is neither hard, straight, or crooked. What am I?

444. I travel in a gaggle. What am I?

445. I have fangs and enjoy piercing holes with a single bite. What am I?

446. Take away my first letter and I remain the same. Take away my last letter, and I remain unchanged. Remove all my letters, and I'm still me. What am I?

447. I come in many shapes and colors. I sing in the breeze but only live 7 months. What am I?

448. I am wingless but airborne, And when I meet your gaze, Tears will fall from your eyes. What am I?

449.	I am like thunder in your cranium. What am I?
450.	A man walks out of a house that has four walls all facing north. A bird walks past him. What is it?
451.	I can sing, but I can't talk. I can climb a high tree, but can't run. I have very soft hair and a very hard mouth. What am I?
452.	What goes round and round the wood but never goes into the wood?
453.	A part of heaven, Though it touches the earth. Some say it's valuable, Others - no worth.
454.	Better old than young; The healthier it is, the smaller it will be.
455.	Blessed are the first. Slow are the second. Playful are the third. Bold are the fourth. Brave are the fifth.

456. A hundred brothers lie next to each other;
Each white and fine - they've only one spine.
I am the tongue that lies between two.
Remove me to gather their wisdom to you.

457. If you are to keep it, you must first give it to me. What is it?

458. I am green for some time, but blue thereafter. If it is dark, I am likely to eat you. What am I?

459. What room can you never enter?

460. I can always go up, never down,
I can always turn left, never right,
I am always hot when I'm cold.

461. Goes over all the hills and hollows,
Bites hard, but never swallows.

462. What has no hands but might knock on your door, and if it does you better open up?

463.	I can sizzle like bacon, I am made with an egg, I have plenty of backbone, But lack a good leg, I peel layers like onions, But still remain whole, I can be long, like a flagpole, Yet fit in a hole.
464.	With my pair I should be, But I am usually alone you see, For a monster always eats me. Do you know what I must be?
465.	Slayer of regrets, old and new, Sought by many, found by few.
466.	A cloud was my mother, the wind is my father, my son is the cool stream, and my daughter is the fruit of the land. A rainbow is my bed, the earth my final resting place, and I'm the torment of man.
467.	A deep well full of knives. What is it?

468. I help you from your head to your toe. The more I work, the smaller I grow. What am I?

469. What is that which goes with a carriage, comes with a carriage, is of no use to a carriage, and yet the carriage cannot go without it?

470. Jimmy is seven years old, and I go everywhere with him. I cast no shadow and breathe no air. I don't weigh anything, and I can't be seen, heard, or touched. Who am I?

471. It's been around for millions of years, But it's no more than a month old.

472. No thicker than your finger when it folds. As thick as what it's holding when it holds.

473. How much dirt is in a hole that's two feet by three feet?

474.	If two's company, and three's a crowd, what are four and five?
475.	When the creeper passes, All the grass kneels.
476.	Where can you finish a book without finishing a sentence?
477.	What must be in the oven yet cannot be baked? Grows in the heat yet shuns the light of day? What sinks in water but rises with air? Looks like skin, but is fine as hair?
478.	If I'm in front, I don't matter, If I'm in back, I make everything be more, I am something, yet I am nothing. What am I?
479.	I shine brightest in the dark. I am there but cannot be seen. To have me costs you nothing. To be without me costs you everything.

480. Spelled forwards,
I'm what you do every day,
Spelled backward,
I'm something you hate.

481. What is put on a table, cut, but never eaten?

482. No head has he but he wears a hat.
No feet has he but he stands up straight.
On him perhaps a fairy sat, weaving a spell
one evening late!

483. Before Mt. Everest was discovered,
what was the highest mountain in the
world?

484. If your uncle's sister is not your aunt,
what relation is she to you?

485. I get sharper the more I'm used.
What am I?

486. What falls but never breaks?
What breaks but never falls?

487.	I have a little house in which I live all alone. It has no doors or windows, and if I want to go out, I must break through the wall.
488.	What can bring tears to your eyes, make you move faster, make you move slower and knock you over?
489.	Always a part, never a whole. If only half grows, I shrink. What am I?
490.	What can cut like a knife, sting like a bee, bite like a lion. Carry truth and lies but never move or speak. What are we?
491.	It's shorter than the rest, but when you're satisfied, you bring it up. What is it?
492.	What breaks every day but can never be fixed?
493.	If a rooster laid a brown egg and a white egg, what kind of chicks would hatch?

494. What sometimes freezes after it has been heated up?

495. What can be swallowed, but can also swallow you?

496. Old Grandpa Diddle Daddle jumped in the mud puddle, green cap and yellow shoes. Guess all your loftiness and you can't guess these news.

497. What two words, added together, contain the most letters?

498. What moves across the land but never has to steer? It has delivered our goods year after year. What is it?

499. I beam, I shine, I sparkle white.
I'll brighten the day with a single light.
I'll charm and enchant all.
I'll bring the best in you all.
What am I?

500.	What word is that, which, deprived of its first letter, leaves you sick?
501.	Imagine that you are in a room with no doors, windows, lights or anything. It's totally dark and silent. You have no phone or flashlight with you. The only things you have with you are the clothes and shoes that you're wearing. How would you get out of this room in 20 seconds?

CONGRATULATIONS

on reaching the end of this book!

So, how did it go?
We hope you enjoyed answering the riddles!
All the answers are on the next pages.

Thank you once again
for choosing our book – your support is truly appreciated!

1. Candle or Pencil	28. Sponge
2. The letter 'm'	29. A river
3. Penny	30. The stars
4. Fence	31. Darkness
5. Joke	32. Bookkeeper
6. Keyboard	33. Charcoal
7. Map	34. Ear of corn
8. Airplane	35. The letter 'c' (sea)
9. Artichoke	36. Fire
10. Echo	37. The letter 'e'
11. Mailbox	38. Time
12. Bottle	39. Fart
13. Cloud	40. Iceberg
14. A Piano	41. Shadow
15. Clock	42. Candle
16. Seesaw	43. Blue
17. Few	44. Icicle
18. Fire	45. Echo
19. Footsteps	46. Music
20. Dice	47. Hole
21. Water	48. Sand
22. Pencil lead	49. The letter 'r'
23. Potato	50. It makes a splash.
24. The Future	51. Teapot
25. Noise	52. Reflection
26. Panda	53. Silence
27. Wind	54. Wholesome

55. Egg

56. Ton

57. It has a snowcap!

58. Fingernail

59. Sands in an hourglass

60. Ace (in a deck of cards)

61. Thorn

62. Pig

63. Towel

64. Splinter

65. Needle and thread

66. Odometer

67. Smile

68. The letter 'n'

69. Rainbow

70. Weary

71. Library

72. House numbers

73. Popcorn

74. The river was frozen.

75. Promise

76. Time

77. School

78. Mirror

79. Full moon

80. Wheel

81. Anchor

82. Stamp

83. Clock

84. Ad-dress

85. It's time to fix the fence!

86. The letter 'e'

87. To the dock-tor

88. Spelling bee!

89. Mount Rushmore

90. On a buzz!

91. Milk truck

92. Chicago

93. He wanted to find his
    friend, Pooh!

94. Because the queen has
    reigned there for years!

95. Cat

96. Queen bee

97. Music

98. Teeth

99. Sleep

100. Because he had no
    body to go with.

101. Hip hop

102. Ten tickles (tentacles)

103. Hummingbird

104. Peacock

105. Snail

106. Racecar

107. Key

108. Deal

109. Blame

110. Your right elbow

111. Because 7 ate 9
     (7, 8, 9)

112. There is no smoke.
     It's an electric train.

113. Nothing

114. The number 8

115. Dictionary

116. E N T (eight, nine, ten)

117. Eat > Ate

118. Bubble

119. One thousand

120. Blueberries

121. Glove

122. The letter 't'

123. Shoe

124. Trouble

125. Egg

126. Wet

127. Seven

128. Wrong

129. Your nose

130. Envelope

131. The letter 'w'

132. Choice

133. Porcupine

134. Every month has 28
     days.

135. Coat of paint

136. River bank

137. In Roman numerals
     (L = 50, XL = 40)

138. Carpet

139. Hippo's shadow

140. Add a "g" and it's
     "gone"

141. Edam

142. A one-story house has
     no stairs.

143. I'm stuck on you!

144. I lava you!

145. Needle

146. Soap

147. Cashew

148. Carpet

149. Door

150. His horse's name is
     Friday.

151. Feather
152. Morning dew
153. SEE O DOUBLE YOU
154. Because it has Greece
     (grease) at the bottom.
155. SWIMS
156. goldfish
157. David
158. Have an ice day!
159. Palm
160. Kite
161. Age
162. The letter "r"
163. Tongs
164. Braids
165. Light
166. Tomorrow
167. Cane
168. Memory
169. Light
170. Your name
171. Jar
172. Mountain
173. Hole
174. Weary
175. Sawdust
176. Road

177. Moon
178. Window
179. Someone's heart
180. Thumb
181. Clock
182. Sandal
183. Cabbage
184. Shrimp
185. Your breath
186. Match
187. Chalkboard
188. Grapes
189. Echo
190. Arrow
191. MISSISSIPPI
192. Fear
193. Thanks
194. NOON
195. Birthday candles
196. Handcuffs
197. Today is her eleventh
     birthday.
198. Doorbell
199. Leaves
200. River
201. Kangaroo
202. Watchdog

203. Telephone
204. Silence
205. Asteroids
206. Flag
207. Jack in the box
208. Broom
209. Toothpaste
210. Letter
211. Temper
212. The letter "i"
213. Oceans
214. Daisy
215. Grow Older or Breathe
216. Bat
217. Teresa's Daughter
218. Web
219. Cold
220. Comb
221. They are grandfather, father, and son.
222. He was walking.
223. Dictionary
224. Lettuce
225. Milk
226. Sister
227. Rainbow
228. Spotlight

229. Watermelon
230. Path
231. Peanut
232. Tissue
233. Coin
234. It happens every year.
235. What's the time?
236. Lost
237. Mirror
238. Roots
239. It's in the middle of "water".
240. Hands
241. Right angle
242. Space
243. Fountain
244. Hourglass
245. Bee
246. Rain
247. Snowflake
248. MONkey, DONkey, TURkey
249. Horizon
250. The letter "r"
251. Potato
252. Receding hare line

253. One. It was not mentioned that the others were going to St. Ives as well.
254. Nothing. It just waved.
255. 12 after 1
256. Heart
257. Wind
258. Time
259. Crane
260. Dream
261. Windmill
262. Reflection
263. Money
264. Knowledge
265. In the dictionary
266. Nice belt!
267. Lint
268. The nose
269. Your teeth
270. Brain
271. Bell
272. Man (life's stages: baby, adult, old age with a cane)
273. Elevator
274. Bulldozer
275. Beard
276. Violin
277. All the people were married.
278. Pillow
279. Carpet
280. Tomorrow
281. Mouth
282. Thoughts
283. Sun
284. Stars
285. Same middle name
286. Watch
287. Steel chain
288. Advice
289. Your breath
290. Outside
291. He's bald.
292. Baking soda
293. Wisdom
294. Meat
295. Frostbite
296. Golf ball
297. Shadow
298. Donkey
299. Garbage truck

300. Fly
301. No one is lying.
The three doctors are
Paul's sisters.
302. Lawsuit
303. By standing
back-to-back with him.
304. Deck of cards.
305. Age
306. A fishhook or the bait
on a fishhook
307. Winter
308. Glasses
309. Watermelon
310. Milky Way
311. Your sister
312. Emojis
313. The letter "d"
314. Volcano
315. Umbrella
316. Seven is the only one
with two syllables.
317. Match
318. Automobile
319. Neither because they
both weigh one pound.
320. Smiles, because there
is a mile between
each 's'.
321. Short
322. Post office
323. 1 brother
324. Queue
325. Ping-pong ball
326. Barber
327. You don't bury the
survivors.
328. February since it's the
shortest month.
329. It was not raining.
330. Umbrella
331. Stairs
332. Mirror
333. Risk
334. They are a
grandfather, father,
and son.
335. Book
336. Traffic light
337. Hurricane

338. Ship
339. Makeup
340. Giraffe
341. Riddle
342. Las Vegas
343. Wheelbarrow
344. Scarecrow
345. Penguin
346. Glasses
347. Chair
348. Vacuum cleaner
349. Zebra
350. Eraser
351. Justice
352. Photograph
353. Doctor
354. Train
355. Cipher
356. Fart
357. Fear
358. Cornfield
359. Computer
360. Plankton
361. Birthday
362. Fleas
363. Jelly
364. Oil

365. Phonebook
366. Triangle
367. Gloves
368. Children
369. Money
370. Plant
371. Beetle
372. Coconut
373. Radio
374. Clone
375. Reflection
376. Sunglasses
377. Light bulb
378. Snowman
379. Chimney
380. Moon
381. Spider
382. Pun
383. Poison
384. Rooster
385. Ladder
386. Mind
387. Teeth
388. Egg
389. Ruler
390. Net

391. Seat belt	418. Comb
392. Eye	419. Fly
393. Bell	420. He's self-employed.
394. Clothes hanger	421. Needle
395. He sleeps at night.	422. Magnet
396. Temper	423. Friendship
397. Time	424. Coffee
398. Paperclip	425. Sunshine
399. Abbreviation	426. Bed
400. Bow	427. Tree
401. Electric fan	428. Knowledge
402. Ivy	429. Halloween
403. Donut	430. Metronome
404. Bellows	431. Puzzle
405. Shadow	432. Guitar
406. Light switch	433. Beehive
407. Secret	434. Sleep
408. The Last Supper	435. Blood
409. Calories	436. Pattern
410. Wine	437. Watch
411. Shoes	438. Calendar
412. Bowling ball	439. Bookworm
413. Tongue	440. Mercury in a thermometer
414. Cricket	441. Breath
415. Oval	442. Baseball
416. Light	
417. Lettuce	

443. Sawdust

444. Goose

445. Stapler

446. Mailman

447. Leaf

448. Smoke

449. Headache

450. Penguin

451. Bird

452. Bark of a tree

453. Rainbow

454. Wound

455. Blade

456. Bookmark

457. Word

458. Grue

459. Mushroom

460. Ski lift

461. Frost

462. Opportunity

463. Snake

464. Socks

465. Redemption

466. Rain

467. Mouth

468. Bar of soap

469. Noise

470. Jimmy's imaginary friend

471. Moon

472. Sack

473. None. It's a hole.

474. Nine

475. Plow

476. Prison

477. Yeast

478. Zero

479. Hope

480. Live

481. Deck of cards

482. Toadstool

483. Still Mt. Everest. It just wasn't discovered yet.

484. Your mother

485. Brain

486. Night and day

487. Chick in an egg

488. Wind

489. Fraction

490. Words

491. Your thumb

492. Dawn

493. Roosters don't lay eggs.

494. Computer

495. Pride

496. Frog

497. Post office

498. Train

499. Smile

500. Music

501. Just stop imagining.

Megan   Matthew

Printed in Great Britain
by Amazon

55923404R00050